Y0-EKT-708

Playtime

A LITTLE SIMON LEARNER

Written by Sue Tarsky
Illustrated by David Bennett

LITTLE SIMON
Published by Simon & Schuster, New York

It's playtime.

playing indoors

playing outdoors

Which do you like best?

Games with balls—

throwing and catching

kicking

rolling

What color are all of these balls?

Everyone is in the playground.

What are they doing?

It's a very hot day.

splashing in the pool

digging in the sand

What do you do on a hot day?

Snow is very cold.

building a snowman

riding a sled

What does snow feel like?

Bricks are for building.

a little tower

a tall tower

a big castle

Who lives in a castle?

You can play hide-and-seek.

How many friends are hiding?

Dressing up is fun.

princess

pirate

rock star

ghost

Who do you pretend to be?

Pretending to be an animal—

sitting like a frog

stretching like a cat

waddling like a duck

pecking like a chicken

What noises do these animals make?

Some toys have wheels.

tricycle

car

What other toys have wheels?

Finding other playthings—

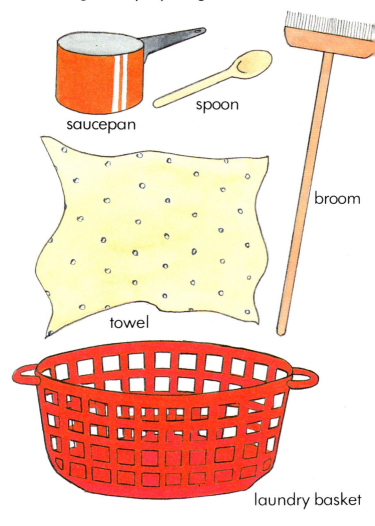

saucepan

spoon

broom

towel

laundry basket

What is everyone playing?

Using your hands to play—

coloring

rolling dough

making a mud pie

painting

making a big mess

How do your hands get messy?

Put away your toys until tomorrow.

animal on the shelf

bricks in the box

Where do your toys go?

's dinnertime.

Have you finished playing?